Presented to:

_____

From:

_____

Date:

_____

Jesus Calling®

FOR

Moms

SARAH YOUNG

THOMAS NELSON
Since 1798

Introduction

Her children arise and call her blessed.

PROVERBS 31:28

Dear Reader,

Mothers are one of God's most grace-filled earthly gifts. Mothers wipe tears, fill hearts, and tend to the needs of their families. They make unseen sacrifices and carry burdens tenderly. A mother's love mirrors God's love in so many ways!

I pray that the pages of this book will offer encouragement and reassurance to your heart. May you feel celebrated for the love, comfort, and strength you provide. God's gifts are abundant, and the greatest treasure He gives us is the priceless gift of His only Son, Jesus.

The devotions in this book are written from the

perspective of Jesus speaking to you, the reader. I have included Scripture with each devotion, and I encourage you to read both—slowly and prayerfully.

I will be praying for you as you read *Jesus Calling for Moms*. For any who do not yet know Jesus as Savior, I'll be asking God to bring you into His family of believers. Remember that Jesus is with you at all times. May you enjoy His presence and His peace in ever-increasing measure.

Bountiful blessings!

Sarah Young

A Prayer for Moms

Compassionate Lord Jesus,

I ask You to use these devotions to bless and help mothers—strengthening, encouraging, and comforting them as they go about their daily lives. Remind them that You are with them each and every moment, regardless of what is happening. Please shower them with Your unfailing Love, and enable them to love their children well. Help their children truly know You as Savior and Lord.

In Your glorious, victorious Name,
Amen

*L*ISTEN TO THE LOVE SONG that I am continually singing to you. *I take great delight in you. I rejoice over you with singing.* The voices of the world are a cacophony of chaos, pulling you this way and that. Don't listen to those voices; challenge them with My Word. Learn to take minibreaks from the world, finding a place to be still in My Presence and listen to My voice.

There is immense hidden treasure to be found through listening to Me. Though I pour out blessings upon you always, some of My richest blessings have to be actively sought. I love to reveal Myself to you, and your seeking heart opens you up to receive more of My disclosure. *Ask and it will be given to you; seek and you will find; knock and the door will be opened to you.*

"The LORD your God is with you, he is mighty to save. He will take great delight in you, he will quiet you with his love, he will rejoice over you with singing."

ZEPHANIAH 3:17

While he was still speaking, a bright cloud enveloped them, and a voice from the cloud said, "This is my Son, whom I love; with him I am well pleased. Listen to him!"

MATTHEW 17:5

"Ask and it will be given to you; seek and you will find; knock and the door will be opened to you."

MATTHEW 7:7

I WANT YOU TO LEARN A NEW HABIT. Try saying, "I trust You, Jesus," in response to whatever happens to you. If there is time, think about who I AM in all My Power and Glory; ponder also the depth and breadth of My Love for you.

This simple practice will help you see Me in every situation, acknowledging My sovereign control over the universe. When you view events from this perspective—through the Light of My universal Presence—fear loses its grip on you. Adverse circumstances become growth opportunities when you affirm your trust in Me no matter what. You receive blessings gratefully, realizing they flow directly from My hand of grace. Your continual assertion of trusting Me will strengthen our relationship and keep you close to Me.

I have seen you in the sanctuary and
beheld your power and your glory.

PSALM 63:2

See, the Sovereign LORD comes with power, and his
arm rules for him. See, his reward is with him, and his
recompense accompanies him. He tends his flock like a
shepherd: he gathers the lambs in his arms and carries them
close to his heart; he gently leads those that have young.

ISAIAH 40:10—11

Where can I go from your Spirit? Where can I flee from your
presence? If I go up to the heavens, you are there; if I make
my bed in the depths, you are there. If I rise on the wings
of the dawn, if I settle on the far side of the sea, even there
your hand will guide me, your right hand will hold me fast.

PSALM 139:7—10

Y LOVE CHASES AFTER YOU every day of your life. So look for signs of My tender Presence as you go through this day. I disclose Myself to you in a vast variety of ways—words of Scripture just when you need them, helpful words spoken through other people, "coincidences" orchestrated by My Spirit, nature's beauty, and so on. My Love for you is not passive; it actively chases after you and leaps into your life. Invite Me to open the eyes of your heart so you can "see" Me blessing you in myriad ways—both small and great.

I want you not only to receive My bountiful blessings but to take careful note of them. Treasure them and *ponder them in your heart.* Thank Me for these ways I show up in your life; write some of them down so you can enjoy them again and again. These signs of My Presence strengthen you and prepare you for difficulties on the road ahead. Remember that *nothing in all creation can separate you from My Love.*

Your beauty and love chase after me every day of my life.
I'm back home in the house of GOD for the rest of my life.

PSALM 23:6 MSG

Your word I have hidden in my heart,
that I might not sin against You.

PSALM 119:11 NKJV

But Mary treasured up all these things
and pondered them in her heart.

LUKE 2:19

Neither height nor depth, nor anything else in
all creation, will be able to separate us from the
love of God that is in Christ Jesus our Lord.

ROMANS 8:39

I MYSELF GO BEFORE YOU AND WILL BE WITH YOU. *So do not be afraid; do not be discouraged.* I, your loving Savior, am also infinite God! I am omnipresent: present everywhere at once. This makes it possible for Me to go ahead of you—opening up the way—without ever leaving your side.

The promise of My Presence is for all time. No matter where you go or what circumstances you encounter, I *will* be with you. This is the basis of your courage and confidence. Though fear and discouragement may sometimes slink into your heart, this is not their rightful home. Your heart is *My* dwelling place, and those hurtful emotions are not from Me. In fact, My *perfect Love casts out fear.* So check your heart from time to time, to see if fear and discouragement are loitering there. If you discover those unwelcome intruders, ask the Holy Spirit to function as a bouncer and boot them out! Then, encourage yourself with My promise to *go before you and be with you*—and let My perfect Love renew your hope.

The LORD himself goes before you and will be
with you; he will never leave you nor forsake you.
Do not be afraid; do not be discouraged.

DEUTERONOMY 31:8

I pray that out of his glorious riches he may strengthen
you with power through his Spirit in your inner being, so
that Christ may dwell in your hearts through faith.

EPHESIANS 3:16–17

There is no fear in love; but perfect love casts
out fear, because fear involves punishment, and
the one who fears is not perfected in love.

1 JOHN 4:18 NASB

"*Remain* in me, and I will remain in you. No branch can bear *fruit* by itself; it must remain in the *vine*. Neither can you bear fruit unless you remain in me."

JOHN 15:4

A Prayer for My Children

_____

_____

_____

_____

_____

_____

_____

_____

_____

_____

_____

_____

O NOT WORRY ABOUT TOMORROW! This is a most gracious command. I understand human frailty; I know that *you are dust*. This command is not meant to burden you or condemn you. It is meant to set you free from worldly cares.

Just before I gave this directive to My followers, I spoke about how to enjoy such freedom. Remember that *your heavenly Father knows what you need*. As you *seek first His kingdom and His righteousness*, your perspective changes. Worldly pursuits become secondary to matters of unseen, eternal reality—the advancement of My kingdom. So put more time and energy into developing your relationship with Me, seeking not only My Presence but also My will. Be ready to follow wherever I lead. I will guide you along adventurous paths that can fill your life with meaning.

I created you to enjoy My Presence in the present— entrusting your future into My care and keeping. As you *delight yourself in Me, I give you the desires of your heart.*

"For the pagans run after all these things, and your heavenly Father knows that you need them. But seek first his kingdom and his righteousness, and all these things will be given to you as well. Therefore do not worry about tomorrow, for tomorrow will worry about itself. Each day has enough trouble of its own."

MATTHEW 6:32–34

For He knows our frame; He remembers that we are dust.

PSALM 103:14 NKJV

Delight yourself in the LORD and he will
give you the desires of your heart.

PSALM 37:4

*C*OME CLOSE TO ME, AND REST IN MY PRESENCE. I am all around you, closer than the very air you breathe. Trust Me with each breath you take.

Your need for Me is as constant as your need for oxygen. So don't neglect the discipline of practicing My Presence. Because your mind is easily distracted, you must keep coming back to Me again and again. Do not be discouraged by your tendency to wander off in tangents from your true Center in Me. Simply keep making the needed adjustments to return to Me. Make these little corrections joyfully—trusting in *My unfailing Love*.

Use My Name, "Jesus," to reconnect with Me. Whisper it, sing it, shout it—remembering what it means: "The Lord saves." Embellish My Name with words of love and trust. Let your heart overflow with gratitude as you ponder all I am to you, all I have done for you. These practices draw you close to Me and help you rest in My Presence.

Find rest, O my soul, in God alone; my hope comes
from him. He alone is my rock and my salvation;
he is my fortress, I will not be shaken.

PSALM 62:5–6

I am like an olive tree flourishing in the house of God;
I trust in God's unfailing love for ever and ever.

PSALM 52:8

She will bring forth a Son, and you shall call His name
JESUS, for He will save His people from their sins.

MATTHEW 1:21 NKJV

*L*ET *M*Y UNFAILING *L*OVE *be your comfort.* "Comfort" eases grief and trouble; it also gives strength and hope. The best source of these blessings is My constant Love that will never, ever fail you. No matter what is happening in your life, this Love can console you and cheer you up. However, you must make the effort to turn to Me for help. I am always accessible to you, and I delight in giving you everything you need.

I have complete, perfect understanding of you and your circumstances. My grasp of your situation is far better than yours. So beware of being overly introspective—trying to figure things out by looking inward, leaving Me out of the equation. When you realize you have done this, turn to Me with a brief prayer: "Help me, Jesus." Remind yourself that *I* am the most important part of the equation of your life! Relax with Me awhile, letting My loving Presence comfort you. *In the world you will have trouble; but be of good cheer, I have overcome the world.*

May your unfailing love be my comfort,
according to your promise to your servant.

PSALM 119:76

The LORD gives strength to his people; the
LORD blesses his people with peace.

PSALM 29:11

Why are you in despair, O my soul? And why have
you become disturbed within me? Hope in God, for I
shall again praise Him for the help of His presence.

PSALM 42:5 NASB

"These things I have *spoken* to you, that in Me you may have *peace*. In the world you will have tribulation; but be of good cheer, I have *overcome* the world."

JOHN 16:33 NKJV

A Prayer for My Children

_____

_____

_____

_____

_____

_____

_____

_____

_____

_____

*Y*OU ARE MINE FOR ALL TIME—and beyond time, into eternity. No power can deny you your inheritance in heaven. I want you to realize how utterly secure you are! Even if you falter as you journey through life, I will never let go of your hand.

Knowing that your future is absolutely assured can free you to live abundantly today. I have prepared this day for you with the most tender concern and attention to detail. Instead of approaching the day as a blank page that you need to fill up, try living it in a responsive mode, being on the lookout for all that I am doing. This sounds easy, but it requires a deep level of trust, based on the knowledge that *My way is perfect.*

Praise be to the God and Father of our Lord Jesus Christ! In his great mercy he has given us new birth into a living hope through the resurrection of Jesus Christ from the dead, and into an inheritance that can never perish, spoil or fade—kept in heaven for you.

1 PETER 1:3–4

If the LORD delights in a man's way, he makes his steps firm; though he stumble, he will not fall, for the LORD upholds him with his hand.

PSALM 37:23–24

As for God, his way is perfect; the word of the LORD is flawless. He is a shield for all who take refuge in him.

PSALM 18:30

*T*RUST ME IN TIMES OF CONFUSION—when things don't make sense and nothing you do seems to help. This type of trust delights Me because I know it is real. Invite Me to enter into your struggles—to be ever so close to you. Though other people may not really understand what you're going through, I understand perfectly. Find comfort in knowing you're not alone in your struggles. *I am with you, watching over you* continually.

Long-term trials can drain you of energy and hope, making it hard for you to keep trusting Me. But I have given you a wonderful *Helper*, the Holy Spirit, who never runs out of strength. You can ask for His help, praying: "I trust You, Jesus; help me, Holy Spirit." Instead of trying to resolve all your problems, simply rest in My Presence. Trust that there is a way forward, even though you can't yet see it. I am providing a good way for you, though it is bumpy at times. When the road is rough, cling all the more tightly to Me. *As your soul clings to Me, My right hand upholds you.*

"I am with you and will watch over you wherever you go, and I will bring you back to this land. I will not leave you until I have done what I have promised you."

GENESIS 28:15

"When the Helper comes, whom I shall send to you from the Father, the Spirit of truth who proceeds from the Father, He will testify of Me."

JOHN 15:26 NKJV

My soul clings to you; your right hand upholds me.

PSALM 63:8

*T*O INFUSE MORE JOY into your day, seek to increase your awareness that I am with you. An easy way to do this is to say: "Thank You, Jesus, for Your Presence." This is such a short, simple prayer that you can pray it frequently; it beautifully connects you to Me, expressing your gratitude. You don't have to *feel* My nearness in order to pray this way. However, the more you thank Me for My Presence, the more real I become to you. You align yourself—mind, heart, and spirit—with the reality that *in Me you live and move and have your being.*

You also increase your awareness by looking for signs of My unseen Presence around you. The beauties of nature and the pleasures of loved ones are reminders, pointing you to Me. You can also find Me in My Word, for I am the living Word. Ask My Spirit to illuminate Scripture to you—shining His Light in your heart, helping you see the Glory of My Presence.

"For in him we live and move and have our being." As some of your own poets have said, "We are his offspring."

ACTS 17:28

In the beginning was the Word, and the
Word was with God, and the Word was God.
He was in the beginning with God.

JOHN 1:1–2 NKJV

For God, who said, "Let light shine out of darkness,"
made his light shine in our hearts to give us the light of
the knowledge of the glory of God in the face of Christ.

2 CORINTHIANS 4:6

I AM AS NEAR AS A WHISPERED PRAYER: listening attentively even to your softest utterance. People who are in love like to be near each other—usually as close as possible. Often they whisper words of endearment to each other, words that no one else can hear. This sort of closeness, with hushed words of love, is always available to you in your relationship with Me. *I am near to all who call on Me*, even if your call is the faintest whisper. This promise is for *all who call on Me in truth*—who know Me as *the Truth*.

Of course, I respond also to silent prayers, but whispering your words can help you feel closer to Me. Hearing your own voice—however faintly—reinforces your connection with Me. It strengthens your awareness of My unseen Presence and draws you into My loving embrace. Although I rarely speak audibly to My children, you can hear My gentle whispers in your heart. Hear Me saying, "I am with you. I love you. *I will never leave you or forsake you."*

The LORD is near to all who call on him,
to all who call on him in truth.

PSALM 145:18

Jesus said to [Thomas], "I am the way, the truth, and the
life. No one comes to the Father except through Me."

JOHN 14:6 NKJV

The LORD said, "Go out and stand on the mountain in
the presence of the LORD, for the LORD is about to pass
by." Then a great and powerful wind tore the mountains
apart and shattered the rocks before the LORD, but the
LORD was not in the wind. After the wind there was an
earthquake, but the LORD was not in the earthquake.
After the earthquake came a fire, but the LORD was not
in the fire. And after the fire came a gentle whisper.

1 KINGS 19:11 12

"*No one* will be able to stand up against you all the days of your *life*. As I was with Moses, so I will be with you; I will *never* leave you nor forsake you."

JOSHUA 1:5

A Prayer for My Children

*R*EST IN MY PRESENCE, allowing Me to take charge of this day. Do not bolt into the day like a racehorse suddenly released. Instead, walk purposefully with Me, letting Me direct your course one step at a time. Thank Me for each blessing along the way; this brings Joy to both you and Me. A grateful heart protects you from negative thinking. Thankfulness enables you to see the abundance I shower upon you daily. Your prayers and petitions are winged into heaven's throne room when they are permeated with thanksgiving. *In everything give thanks, for this is My will for you.*

"Come to Me, all you who labor and are heavy laden, and I will give you rest."

MATTHEW 11:28 NKJV

Devote yourselves to prayer, being watchful and thankful.

COLOSSIANS 4:2

In everything give thanks; for this is God's will for you in Christ Jesus.

1 THESSALONIANS 5:18 NASB

I AM IMMANUEL—*GOD WITH YOU*—and I am enough! When things in your life are flowing smoothly, it is easy to trust in My sufficiency. However, when you encounter rough patches—one after another after another—you may sometimes feel that My provision is inadequate. This is when your mind tends to go into high gear: obsessing about ways to make things better. There is nothing wrong with seeking solutions, but problem-solving can turn into an addiction: your mind spinning with so many plans and possibilities that you become confused and exhausted.

To protect yourself from this mental exhaustion, you need to remind yourself that *I am with you always*, taking care of you. It is possible to *rejoice in Me*—to proclaim My sufficiency—even during the most difficult times. This is a supernatural work, empowered by My Spirit who lives in you. It is also a decision that you make—day by day and moment by moment. Choose to *be joyful in Me, your Savior*, for I am indeed enough!

"She will bring forth a Son, and you shall call His name Jesus, for He will save His people from their sins." So all this was done that it might be fulfilled which was spoken by the Lord through the prophet, saying: "Behold, the virgin shall be with child, and bear a Son, and they shall call His name Immanuel," which is translated, "God with us."

MATTHEW 1:21–23 NKJV

"[Go and make disciples,] teaching them to obey everything I have commanded you. And surely I am with you always, to the very end of the age."

MATTHEW 28:20

Though the fig tree does not bud and there are no grapes on the vines, though the olive crop fails and the fields produce no food, though there are no sheep in the pen and no cattle in the stalls, yet I will rejoice in the LORD, I will be joyful in God my Savior.

HABAKKUK 3:17–18

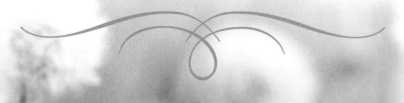

I SPEAK TO YOU CONTINUALLY. My nature is to communicate, though not always in words. I fling glorious sunsets across the sky, day after day after day. I speak in the faces and voices of loved ones. I caress you with a gentle breeze that refreshes and delights you. I speak softly in the depths of your spirit, where I have taken up residence.

You can find Me in each moment, when you have eyes that see and ears that hear. Ask My Spirit to sharpen your spiritual eyesight and hearing. I rejoice each time you discover My Presence. Practice looking and listening for Me during quiet intervals. Gradually you will find Me in more and more of your moments. *You will seek Me and find Me, when you seek Me above all else.*

O Lord, our Lord, how majestic is your name in all the earth! You have set your glory above the heavens. From the lips of children and infants you have ordained praise because of your enemies, to silence the foe and the avenger. When I consider your heavens, the work of your fingers, the moon and the stars, which you have set in place, what is man that you are mindful of him, the son of man that you care for him?

PSALM 8:1—4

The heavens declare the glory of God; the skies proclaim the work of his hands. Day after day they pour forth speech; night after night they display knowledge.

PSALM 19:1—2

Do you not know that your body is a temple of the Holy Spirit, who is in you, whom you have received from God? You are not your own.

1 CORINTHIANS 6:19

"You will *seek* me and find me when you seek me with all your *heart*."

JEREMIAH 29:13

A Prayer for My Children

*Y*OU ARE FEELING WEIGHED DOWN by yesterday's failures. You wish you could undo decisions you made that you now regret. However, the past is beyond the realm of change and cannot be undone. Even *I*, though I live in timelessness, respect the boundaries of time that exist in your world. So don't waste your energy bemoaning bad choices you have made. Instead, ask Me to forgive your sins and help you learn from your mistakes.

I hate to see My children weighed down by past failures, dragging them around like heavy chains attached to their legs. When you're feeling this way, try to imagine Me cutting the chains from your legs. I came to set My loved ones free. You are *free indeed*!

Rejoice that I redeem your failures—forgiving you and leading you along paths of newness. Talk with Me about your mistakes and be ready to *learn from Me*. Ask Me to show you the changes I want you to make. I will *guide you along right paths*.

"Come to me, all you who are weary and burdened, and I will give you rest. Take my yoke upon you and learn from me, for I am gentle and humble in heart, and you will find rest for your souls."

MATTHEW 11:28–29

"Therefore if the Son makes you free, you shall be free indeed."

JOHN 8:36 NKJV

He renews my strength. He guides me along right paths, bringing honor to his name.

PSALM 23:3 NLT

*L*ET MY LOVE ENFOLD YOU in the radiance of My Glory. Sit still in the Light of My Presence, and receive My Peace. These quiet moments with Me transcend time, accomplishing far more than you can imagine. Bring Me the sacrifice of your time, and watch to see how abundantly I bless you and your loved ones.

Through the intimacy of our relationship, you are *being transformed* from the inside out. As you keep your focus on Me, I form you into the one I desire you to be. Your part is to yield to My creative work in you, neither resisting it nor trying to speed it up. Enjoy the tempo of a God-breathed life by letting Me set the pace. Hold My hand in childlike trust, and the way before you will open up step by step.

Through Jesus, therefore, let us continually offer to God a sacrifice of praise—the fruit of lips that confess his name.

HEBREWS 13:15

And we, who with unveiled faces all reflect
the Lord's glory, are being transformed into
his likeness with ever-increasing glory, which
comes from the Lord, who is the Spirit.

2 CORINTHIANS 3:18

Yet I am always with you; you hold me by my
right hand. You guide me with your counsel,
and afterward you will take me into glory.

PSALM 73:23—24

*I*N QUIETNESS AND CONFIDENCE *shall be your strength.* When you're in a tough situation, your mind tends to go into overdrive. You mentally rehearse possible solutions at breakneck speed. Your brain becomes a flurry of activity! You scrutinize your own abilities and those of people you might call upon for help. If you find no immediate solution to your problem, you start to feel anxious. When you find this happening, return to Me and rest *in quietness.* Take time to seek My Face and My will rather than rushing ahead without clear direction.

I want you to have confidence in Me and My ways—patiently trusting in Me even when you can't see the way forward. Whereas anxious striving drains you of energy, quiet confidence will give you strength. You can trust that I will not forsake you in your time of need. Keep communicating with Me about your situation, and be willing to wait—without pushing for immediate resolution. *Those who wait for the Lord will gain new strength.*

Thus says the Lord God, the Holy One of Israel: "In returning and rest you shall be saved; in quietness and confidence shall be your strength."

ISAIAH 30:15 NKJV

Be strong and courageous. Do not be afraid or terrified because of them, for the Lord your God goes with you; he will never leave you nor forsake you.

DEUTERONOMY 31:6

Those who wait for the Lord will gain new strength; they will mount up with wings like eagles, they will run and not get tired, they will walk and not become weary.

ISAIAH 40:31 NASB

*L*OVE IS PATIENT. In the apostle Paul's long list of characteristics of Christian love, the very first one is "patience." This is the ability to endure adversity calmly—not becoming upset when waiting a long time or dealing with difficult people or problems. Paul's emphasis on patience is countercultural, and it is often overlooked by My followers. This vital virtue rarely comes first in people's minds when they think about love. However, there is one common exception to this rule: a devoted mother or father. The demands of babies and young children help develop patience in good parents. They put aside their own needs to focus on their children—tenderly taking care of their needs.

I want My followers to lace their love for one another with plenty of patience. This virtue is the fourth trait listed in the fruit of the Spirit. Therefore, My Spirit can equip you to succeed in this challenging endeavor. Remember that I love you with perfect, *unfailing Love.* Ask the Holy Spirit to help you care for others with My bountiful, patient Love.

Love is patient, love is kind. It does not envy,
it does not boast, it is not proud.

1 CORINTHIANS 13:4

Rejoice in hope; be patient in affliction; be persistent in prayer.

ROMANS 12:12 HCSB

But the fruit of the Spirit is love, joy, peace, patience,
kindness, goodness, faithfulness, gentleness, self-
control; against such things there is no law.

GALATIANS 5:22–23 NASB

The LORD *delights* in those who fear him, who put their *hope* in his unfailing *love*.

PSALM 147:11

A Prayer for My Children

_____

_____

_____

_____

_____

_____

_____

_____

_____

_____

_____

_____

*W*HEN YOU TRUST IN ME, YOU TAKE REFUGE IN ME. So trusting Me is much more than a matter of your words; it is mainly a matter of your will. As you go through this day, you will encounter many things that can make you anxious, including some of your thoughts. If you don't stay alert, anxious feelings can slip into your day without your noticing them. When this happens, you may wonder why you suddenly start to feel bad. Usually, you just ignore those feelings. Or you may try to numb them with food, drink, television, gossip, or other distractions. How much better it is to "catch" the worry-thoughts before they take hold of you. That is why I say, *"Be on the alert!"*

If you are watchful and alert, you can choose to take refuge in Me whenever anxiety comes at you. A refuge is a place that provides protection or shelter: a safe haven. It is something you turn to for help, relief, or escape. I am eager to be your Refuge, and I am with you at all times. Nonetheless, you must exert your will by turning to Me for help. Thus, you make Me your refuge, demonstrating your trust in Me. *Blessed—happy, to be envied—is the one who takes refuge in Me.*

Be of sober spirit, be on the alert. Your adversary, the devil, prowls around like a roaring lion, seeking someone to devour.

1 PETER 5:8 NASB

Be merciful to me, O God, be merciful to me! For my soul trusts in You; and in the shadow of Your wings I will make my refuge, until these calamities have passed by.

PSALM 57:1 NKJV

O taste and see that the Lord [our God] is good! Blessed (happy, fortunate, to be envied) is the man who trusts and takes refuge in Him.

PSALM 34:8 AMPC

I AM PLEASED WITH YOU, MY CHILD. Allow yourself to become fully aware of My pleasure shining upon you. You don't have to perform well in order to receive My Love. In fact, a performance focus will pull you away from Me, toward some sort of Pharisaism. This can be a subtle form of idolatry: worshiping your own good works. It can also be a source of deep discouragement when your works don't measure up to your expectations.

Shift your focus from your performance to My radiant Presence. The Light of My Love shines on you continually, regardless of your feelings or behavior. Your responsibility is to be receptive to this unconditional Love. Thankfulness and trust are your primary receptors. Thank Me for everything; *trust in Me at all times.* These simple disciplines will keep you open to My loving Presence.

For it is by grace you have been saved, through faith—and this not from yourselves, it is the gift of God—not by works, so that no one can boast.

EPHESIANS 2:8–9

I pray that out of his glorious riches he may strengthen you with power through his Spirit in your inner being, so that Christ may dwell in your hearts through faith. And I pray that you, being rooted and established in love, may have power, together with all the saints, to grasp how wide and long and high and deep is the love of Christ, and to know this love that surpasses knowledge—that you may be filled to the measure of all the fullness of God.

EPHESIANS 3:16–19

Trust in him at all times, O people; pour out your hearts to him, for God is our refuge.

PSALM 62:8

I AM CALLING YOU to live in joyful dependence on Me. Many people view dependence as a despicable condition, so they strive to be as self-sufficient as possible. This is not My way for you! I designed you to need Me continually—and to delight in that neediness. When you live in harmony with your Creator's intentions for you, you can maximize your potential and enjoy your life more.

The apostle Paul exhorted Christians to *be joyful always* and to *pray continually*. There is always Joy to be found in My Presence, and I have promised I will *not leave you or forsake you*. So you can speak to Me at all times, knowing that I hear and I care. Praying continually is a way of demonstrating your deliberate dependence on Me—the One to whom you pray. Another powerful way of relying on Me is studying My Word, asking Me to use it to transform you through and through. These delightful disciplines help you live in joyful dependence on Me. *Delight yourself in Me* more and more; this increases your Joy and glorifies Me.

Be joyful always; pray continually.

1 THESSALONIANS 5:16–17

The LORD, He is the One who goes before you.
He will be with you, He will not leave you nor
forsake you; do not fear nor be dismayed.

DEUTERONOMY 31:8 NKJV

With my whole heart I have sought You; oh, let me not
wander from Your commandments! Your word I have
hidden in my heart, that I might not sin against You.
Blessed are You, O LORD! Teach me Your statutes.

PSALM 119:10–12 NKJV

Delight yourself in the LORD and he will give you the desires of your *heart*.

PSALM 37:4

A Prayer for My Children

_____

_____

_____

_____

_____

_____

_____

_____

_____

_____

_____

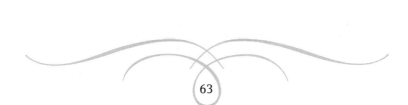

*F*IND ME in the midst of the maelstrom. Sometimes events whirl around you so quickly that they become a blur. Whisper My Name in recognition that I am still with you. Without skipping a beat in the activities that occupy you, you find strength and Peace through praying My Name. Later, when the happenings have run their course, you can talk with Me more fully.

Accept each day just as it comes to you. Do not waste your time and energy wishing for a different set of circumstances. Instead, trust Me enough to yield to My design and purposes. Remember that nothing can separate you from My loving Presence; *you are Mine.*

Therefore God exalted him to the highest place and gave him the name that is above every name, that at the name of Jesus every knee should bow, in heaven and on earth and under the earth, and every tongue confess that Jesus Christ is Lord, to the glory of God the Father.

PHILIPPIANS 2:9–11

The LORD gives strength to his people; the LORD blesses his people with peace.

PSALM 29:11

But now, this is what the LORD says—he who created you, O Jacob, he who formed you, O Israel: "Fear not, for I have redeemed you; I have summoned you by name; you are mine."

ISAIAH 43:1

ON'T BE AFRAID TO BE HAPPY. Because you are Mine, you can expect to experience some happiness—even in this broken world. Yet anxiety sometimes intrudes upon your carefree moments. You start wondering if there are things you should be doing or plans you should be making. Your underlying feeling is that it isn't safe to let down your guard and simply be happy in the moment. How wrong this is, My child!

I have called you to *cease striving*—let go, relax—*and know that I am God*. You may think that you need to have all your ducks in a row before you can relax and enjoy My Presence. But consider the overall context of this command: *though the earth give way and the mountains fall into the heart of the sea*. The psalmist who penned these words was describing a terrifying catastrophe. So you don't need to wait till you've solved all the problems in your life; this very moment is the right time to enjoy Me. Come boldly into My Presence, saying, "Jesus, I choose to enjoy You—here and now."

Happy are the people whose God is the LORD!

PSALM 144:15 NKJV

Cease striving and know that I am God; I will be exalted among the nations, I will be exalted in the earth.

PSALM 46:10 NASB

GOD is our refuge and strength, an ever-present help in trouble. Therefore we will not fear, though the earth give way and the mountains fall into the heart of the sea, though its waters roar and foam and the mountains quake with their surging.

PSALM 46:1–3

EJOICE ALWAYS! This is one of the shortest verses in the Bible, but it is radiant with heavenly Light. I made you in My image, and I crafted you with the ability to choose Joy in the moments of your life. When your mind is going down an unpleasant, gloomy path, stop it in its tracks with this glorious command. See how many times each day you can remind yourself to rejoice.

It is important not only to be joyful but to think about specific reasons for rejoicing. They can be as simple as My daily provisions for you—food, shelter, clothing. Relationships with loved ones can also be a rich source of Joy. Since you are My beloved, your relationship with Me is an ever-present wellspring of gladness. These joyful thoughts will light up both your mind and your heart, enabling you to find more pleasure in your life.

Choosing to rejoice will bless you and those around you. It will also strengthen your relationship with Me.

Rejoice always.

1 THESSALONIANS 5:16 NKJV

So God created man in His own image; in the image of
God He created him; male and female He created them.

GENESIS 1:27 NKJV

Rejoice in the Lord always. I will say it again: Rejoice!

PHILIPPIANS 4:4

*L*EARN TO LAUGH at yourself more freely. Don't take yourself or your circumstances so seriously. Relax and know that I am *God with you.* When you desire My will above all else, life becomes much less threatening. Stop trying to monitor My responsibilities—things that are beyond your control. Find freedom by accepting the boundaries of your domain.

Laughter lightens your load and lifts your heart into heavenly places. Your laughter rises to heaven and blends with angelic melodies of praise. Just as parents delight in the laughter of their children, so I delight in hearing My children laugh. I rejoice when you trust Me enough to enjoy your life lightheartedly.

Do not miss the Joy of My Presence by carrying the weight of the world on your shoulders. Rather, *take My yoke upon you and learn from Me. My yoke is comfortable and pleasant; My burden is light and easily borne.*

A cheerful heart is good medicine, but a
crushed spirit dries up the bones.

PROVERBS 17:22

She is clothed with strength and dignity;
she can laugh at the days to come.

PROVERBS 31:25

Take My yoke upon you and learn of Me, for I am
gentle (meek) and humble (lowly) in heart, and
you will find rest . . . for your souls. For My yoke is
wholesome (useful, good—not harsh, hard, sharp, or
pressing, but comfortable, gracious, and pleasant),
and My burden is light and easy to be borne.

MATTHEW 11:29—30 AMPC

"The virgin will be with *child* and will give birth to a son, and they will call him *Immanuel*"– which means, "*God* with us."

MATTHEW 1:23

A Prayer for My Children

*L*EAN ON ME as you face the circumstances of this day. Whether or not they realize it, all people lean on—depend on—*something*: physical strength, intelligence, beauty, wealth, achievements, family, friends, and so on. All of these are gifts from Me, to be enjoyed gratefully. However, relying on any of these things is risky because every one of them can let you down.

When your circumstances are challenging and you are feeling weak, you tend to obsess about how you are going to make it through the day. This wastes a lot of time and energy; it also distracts you from Me. Whenever this happens, ask Me to open your eyes so you can find Me in the moment. "See" Me standing nearby, with My strong arm extended toward you— offering you My help. Don't try to pretend that you have it all together or that you're stronger than you really are. Instead, lean hard on Me, letting Me bear most of your weight and help you with your problems. Rejoice in Me—*your Strength*—and worship while leaning on Me.

A man of many companions may come to ruin, but there is a friend who sticks closer than a brother.

PROVERBS 18:24

But I will sing of your strength, in the morning I will sing of your love; for you are my fortress, my refuge in times of trouble. O my Strength, I sing praise to you; you, O God, are my fortress, my loving God.

PSALM 59:16—17

By faith Jacob, when he was dying, blessed each of the sons of Joseph, and worshiped, leaning on the top of his staff.

HEBREWS 11:21 NKJV

HEN ANXIETY IS GREAT WITHIN YOU, turn to Me for *consolation*. Other words for "consolation" are *comfort, compassion, empathy, help, encouragement, reassurance*, and *relief*. I gladly provide all of this—and much more—for My children. Yet your natural tendency when you're feeling anxious is to focus on yourself or your problems. The more you do this, the more you forget about Me and all the help I can supply. This worldly focus only increases your anxiety! Let the discomfort you feel at such times alert you to your neglect of Me. Whisper My Name, and invite Me into your difficulties.

Seek My Face, finding comfort in My compassion and empathy. Look to Me for encouragement, reassurance, and help. I know all about your problems, and I also know the best way to deal with them. As you relax in My loving Presence, I strengthen you and provide relief from your anxiety. I reassure you that *nothing in all creation can separate you from My Love*. My consolation is full of blessings, beloved; *it brings Joy to your soul*.

When anxiety was great within me, your
consolation brought joy to my soul.

PSALM 94:19

When You said, "Seek My face," My heart said
to You, "Your face, LORD, I will seek."

PSALM 27:8 NKJV

For I am convinced that neither death nor life, neither
angels nor demons, neither the present nor the future,
nor any powers, neither height nor depth, nor anything
else in all creation, will be able to separate us from
the love of God that is in Christ Jesus our Lord.

ROMANS 8:38–39

*R*EMEMBER *ME ON YOUR BED; think of Me through the watches of the night.* When you are wakeful during the night, thoughts can fly at you from all directions. Unless you take charge of them, you are likely to become anxious. Your best strategy is to think about *Me* during your night watches. Start communicating with Me about whatever is on your mind. *Cast all your anxiety on Me because I care for you.* I am taking care of you! This makes it possible for you to relax and *rejoice in the shadow of My wings.*

When you remember Me during the night, think about who I really am. Ponder My perfections: My Love, Joy, and Peace. Rejoice in My majesty, wisdom, grace, and mercy. Find comfort in My names: Shepherd, Savior, Immanuel, Prince of Peace. Be awed by My Power and Glory, for I am King of kings and Lord of lords. Thus you worship Me and enjoy My Presence. These thoughts of Me will clear your mind—helping you see things from My perspective—and refresh your entire being.

On my bed I remember you; I think of you
through the watches of the night.

PSALM 63:6

Cast all your anxiety on [God] because he cares for you.

1 PETER 5:7

Fight the good fight of the faith. Take hold of the eternal
life to which you were called. . . . I charge you to keep
this command without spot or blame until the appearing
of our Lord Jesus Christ, which God will bring about in
his own time—God, the blessed and only Ruler, the King
of kings and Lord of lords, who alone is immortal and
who lives in unapproachable light, whom no one has
seen or can see. To him be honor and might forever.

1 TIMOTHY 6:12, 14—16

Because You have been my
help, therefore in the shadow
of Your *wings* I will rejoice.

PSALM 63:7 NKJV

A Prayer for My Children

_____

_____

_____

_____

_____

_____

_____

_____

_____

_____

_____

*T*RUST ME by relinquishing control into My hands. *Let go, and recognize that I am God.* This is My world: I made it and I control it. Yours is a responsive part in the litany of Love. I search among My children for receptivity to Me. Guard well this gift that I have planted in your heart. Nurture it with the Light of My Presence.

When you bring Me prayer requests, lay out your concerns before Me. Speak to Me candidly; pour out your heart. Then thank Me for the answers that I have set into motion long before you can discern results. When your requests come to mind again, continue to thank Me for the answers that are on the way. If you keep on stating your concerns to Me, you will live in a state of tension. When you thank Me for how I am answering your prayers, your mind-set becomes much more positive. Thankful prayers keep your focus on My Presence and My promises.

Let be and be still, and know (recognize and understand) that I am God. I will be exalted among the nations! I will be exalted in the earth!

PSALM 46:10 AMPC

Devote yourselves to prayer, being watchful and thankful.

COLOSSIANS 4:2

His divine power has given us everything we need for life and godliness through our knowledge of him who called us by his own glory and goodness. Through these he has given us his very great and precious promises, so that through them you may participate in the divine nature and escape the corruption in the world caused by evil desires.

2 PETER 1:3–4

*C*OME TO ME, My weary one. Find rest in My refreshing Presence. I am always by your side, eager to help you— but sometimes you are forgetful of Me.

You are easily distracted by the demands of other people. Their expectations can be expressed in ways that are harsh or gentle, guilt-inducing or kind. But if these demands are numerous and weighty, they eventually add up to a crushing load.

When you find yourself sinking under *heavy burdens*, turn to Me for help. Ask Me to lift those weights from your shoulders and carry them for you. Talk with Me about the matters that concern you. Let the Light of My Presence shine on them so you can see the way forward. This same Light soothes and strengthens you as it soaks into the depths of your being.

Open your heart to My healing, holy Presence. *Lift up your hands* in joyful adoration, letting My blessings flow freely into you. Take time to rest with Me, beloved; relax while I *bless you with Peace.*

Then Jesus said, "Come to me, all of you who are weary and carry heavy burdens, and I will give you rest."

MATTHEW 11:28 NLT

Lift up your hands in the sanctuary and praise the LORD.

PSALM 134:2

The LORD gives strength to his people; the LORD blesses his people with peace.

PSALM 29:11

*S*TOP YOUR INCESSANT WORRY-PLANNING! Draw your mind back from the future to the present moment, where My Presence lovingly awaits you. *Seek My Face* with a smile in your heart, knowing that I take delight in you. Talk with Me about all that concerns you and the tasks that are weighing on you. Call out to Me for help as you set priorities according to My will. Then keep returning your focus to Me and to the work at hand. Inviting Me into your activities increases your Joy and helps you to be more effective.

When you need to take a break, remember that I am your resting place. My *everlasting arms* are always available to support you and hold you close. When you relax in My company—waiting with Me for a time—this demonstrates genuine trust in Me. As you prepare to return to your tasks, make the effort to include *Me* in your plans. This protects you from worrying; it also helps you stay close to Me, enjoying My Presence.

"Who of you by worrying can add a single hour to his life? Since you cannot do this very little thing, why do you worry about the rest?"

LUKE 12:25–26

When You said, "Seek My face," my heart said to You, "Your face, LORD, I will seek."

PSALM 27:8 NKJV

Find rest, O my soul, in God alone; my hope comes from him. He alone is my rock and my salvation; he is my fortress, I will not be shaken.

PSALM 62:5–6

The *eternal* God is your refuge, and underneath are the *everlasting* arms.

DEUTERONOMY 33:27

A Prayer for My Children

_____

_____

_____

_____

_____

_____

_____

_____

_____

_____

_____

*B*EWARE OF SEEING YOURSELF through other people's eyes. There are several dangers to this practice. First of all, it is nearly impossible to discern what others actually think of you. Moreover, their views of you are variable: subject to each viewer's spiritual, emotional, and physical condition. The major problem with letting others define you is that it borders on idolatry. Your concern to please others dampens your desire to please Me, your Creator.

It is much more real to see yourself through *My eyes*. My gaze upon you is steady and sure, untainted by sin. Through My eyes you can see yourself as one who is deeply, eternally loved. Rest in My loving gaze, and you will receive deep Peace. Respond to My loving Presence by *worshiping Me in spirit and in truth*.

And without faith it is impossible to please God, because
anyone who comes to him must believe that he exists
and that he rewards those who earnestly seek him.

HEBREWS 11:6

And hope does not disappoint us, because
God has poured out his love into our hearts by
the Holy Spirit, whom he has given us.

ROMANS 5:5

"Yet a time is coming and has now come when the
true worshipers will worship the Father in spirit
and truth, for they are the kind of worshipers the
Father seeks. God is spirit, and his worshipers
must worship in spirit and in truth."

JOHN 4:23–24

*T*AKE TIME TO *MEDITATE ON MY UNFAILING LOVE. For I am your God forever and ever; I will be your Guide even to the end.* Ask the Holy Spirit to help you meditate on My loving Presence—to bring your mind back to Me whenever it wanders. Encourage yourself with the words of the patriarch Jacob: "Surely the Lord is in this place." Rejoice that I am your God forevermore—today, tomorrow, and throughout all eternity.

I am also your Guide. It is easy to be spooked by the future when you forget that I am leading you each step along your life-path. Ever since you trusted Me as Savior, My guiding Presence has been available to you. I am training you to be increasingly aware of Me as you go about your daily activities. You can draw near Me at any time simply by whispering My Name. Later, when you have more time, bring Me *your prayer and supplication with thanksgiving.* Relax in the wondrous assurance that I am *your Guide even to the end.*

Within your temple, O God, we meditate on your unfailing love. Like your name, O God, your praise reaches to the ends of the earth; your right hand is filled with righteousness. . . . For this God is our God for ever and ever; he will be our guide even to the end.

PSALM 48:9–10, 14

When Jacob awoke from his sleep, he thought, "Surely the LORD is in this place, and I was not aware of it."

GENESIS 28:16

Be anxious for nothing, but in everything by prayer and supplication, with thanksgiving, let your requests be made known to God; and the peace of God, which surpasses all understanding, will guard your hearts and minds through Christ Jesus.

PHILIPPIANS 4:6–7 NKJV

I AM WORTHY of all your confidence, all your trust. So refuse to let world events spook you. Instead, pour your energy into trusting Me and looking for evidence of My Presence in the world. Whisper My Name to reconnect your heart and mind to Me quickly. *I am near to all who call upon Me.* Let Me wrap you up in My abiding Presence and comfort you with My Peace.

Remember that I am both loving and faithful. *My Love reaches to the heavens, My faithfulness to the skies*! This means you can never come to the end of My Love. It is limitless and everlasting. Moreover, you can stand on the Rock of My faithfulness, no matter what circumstances you may be facing.

People routinely put their confidence in their abilities, education, wealth, or appearance. But I urge you to place your confidence fully in Me—the Savior whose sacrificial death and miraculous resurrection opened the way for you into *eternal Glory*!

The Lord is near to all who call upon Him,
to all who call upon Him in truth.

PSALM 145:18 NKJV

Your love, O Lord, reaches to the heavens,
your faithfulness to the skies.

PSALM 36:5

For our light and momentary troubles are achieving
for us an eternal glory that far outweighs them all.

2 CORINTHIANS 4:17

I CONTINUALLY CALL YOU to closeness with Me. I know the depth and breadth of your need for Me. I can read the emptiness of your thoughts when they wander away from Me. I offer rest for your soul, as well as refreshment for your mind and body. As you increasingly find fulfillment in Me, other pleasures become less important. Knowing Me intimately is like having a private wellspring of Joy within you. This spring flows freely from My throne of grace, so your Joy is independent of circumstances.

Waiting in My Presence keeps you connected to Me, aware of all that I offer you. If you feel any deficiency, you need to refocus your attention on Me. This is how you trust Me in the moments of your life.

But I have stilled and quieted my soul; like a weaned child with its mother, like a weaned child is my soul within me.

PSALM 131:2

Surely you have granted him eternal blessings and made him glad with the joy of your presence.

PSALM 21:6

Be still before the LORD and wait patiently for him; do not fret when men succeed in their ways, when they carry out their wicked schemes.

PSALM 37:7

But *blessed* are those who trust
in the Lᴏʀᴅ and have made the
Lord their hope and *confidence*.

Jᴇʀᴇᴍɪᴀʜ 17:7 ɴʟᴛ

A Prayer for My Children

_____

_____

_____

_____

_____

_____

_____

_____

_____

_____

_____

_____

I WANT YOU TO RELAX and enjoy this day. It's easy for you to get so focused on your goals that you push yourself too hard— and neglect your need for rest. You tend to judge yourself on the basis of how much you've accomplished. There is certainly a time and place for being productive, using the opportunities and abilities I provide. Nonetheless, I want you to be able to like yourself as much when you're relaxing as when you're achieving.

Rest in the knowledge that you're a child of God, *saved by grace through faith* in Me. This is your ultimate—and foundational—identity. You hold a position of royalty in My eternal kingdom. Remember who you are!

When you're comfortable enough in your true identity to balance work with relaxation, you are more effective in My kingdom. A refreshed mind is able to think more clearly and biblically. A *restored soul* is more winsome and loving in interactions with others. So take time with Me, and let Me *lead you beside waters of rest.*

By the seventh day God had finished the work he had been doing; so on the seventh day he rested from all his work. And God blessed the seventh day and made it holy, because on it he rested from all the work of creating that he had done.

GENESIS 2:2–3

For by grace you have been saved through faith, and that not of yourselves; it is the gift of God.

EPHESIANS 2:8 NKJV

He makes me lie down in green pastures; He leads me beside quiet waters. He restores my soul; He guides me in the paths of righteousness for His name's sake.

PSALM 23:2–3 NASB

Trust Me, and don't be afraid. Many things feel out of control. Your routines are not running smoothly. You tend to feel more secure when your life is predictable. Let Me lead you to *the rock that is higher than you* and your circumstances. *Take refuge in the shelter of My wings*, where you are absolutely secure.

When you are shaken out of your comfortable routines, grip My hand tightly and look for growth opportunities. Instead of bemoaning the loss of your comfort, accept the challenge of something new. *I lead you on from glory to glory*, making you fit for My kingdom. Say *yes* to the ways I work in your life. Trust Me, and don't be afraid.

Surely God is my salvation; I will trust and not
be afraid. The LORD, the LORD, is my strength
and my song; he has become my salvation.

ISAIAH 12:2

From the ends of the earth I call to you, I call as my
heart grows faint; lead me to the rock that is higher
than I. For you have been my refuge, a strong tower
against the foe. I long to dwell in your tent forever
and take refuge in the shelter of your wings.

PSALM 61:2–4

But we all, with unveiled face, beholding as in a mirror
the glory of the Lord, are being transformed into the same
image from glory to glory, just as by the Spirit of the Lord.

2 CORINTHIANS 3:18 NKJV

*R*EJOICE THAT I UNDERSTAND YOU completely and love you with perfect, unending Love. Many people are afraid that anyone who comes to know them fully will look down on them or even reject them. So they strive to keep others at a safe distance, disclosing only the parts of themselves they think are acceptable. This way of interacting with others tends to feel safer, but it leads to loneliness.

Be thankful that there is One who sees straight through your defenses and pretenses. There is no hiding from Me! I know absolutely *everything* about you. So rest in the wonder of being *fully known*—yet delighted in! You don't have to work at trying to earn My Love. The truth is, nothing could ever *stop* Me from loving you. Because you are Mine—bought with My blood—you are accepted and treasured forever. You need to tell yourself this truth over and over, till it seeps into your inner being and changes the way you view yourself. Self-acceptance is the path to self-forgetfulness, which is the royal road to Joy!

Oh give thanks to the LORD, for he is good, for
his steadfast love endures forever! . . . Whoever
is wise, let him attend to these things; let them
consider the steadfast love of the LORD.

PSALM 107:1, 43 ESV

Now we see but a poor reflection as in a mirror; then
we shall see face to face. Now I know in part; then
I shall know fully, even as I am fully known.

1 CORINTHIANS 13:12

Having predestined us to adoption as sons by Jesus
Christ to Himself, according to the good pleasure
of His will, to the praise of the glory of His grace,
by which He made us accepted in the Beloved.

EPHESIANS 1:5—6 NKJV

For the LORD takes *delight* in his people; he crowns the humble with *salvation*. Let the saints rejoice in this honor and sing for *joy* on their beds.

PSALM 149:4–5

A Prayer for My Children

*L*ET *MY COMFORTS DELIGHT YOUR SOUL.* The world presents you with *a multitude of anxieties*—too numerous for you to count. Everywhere you turn, you see problems and trouble. In the midst of this mess, look to Me for help. Whisper My Name, "Jesus," thus reactivating your awareness of My Presence. Your perspective changes dramatically as My Presence comes onto the screen of your consciousness, lighting up your worldview. My comforts can soothe your troubled heart and delight your soul.

If the world were perfect, you would never experience the pleasure of receiving comfort from Me. Instead of letting problems discourage you, use them as reminders to seek Me— My Presence, My Peace, My Love. These invisible realities are available to you any time, any place, and they provide Joy that no one can take away from you. So *come to Me when you are weary and burdened*; I will provide *rest for your soul.*

In the multitude of my anxieties within
me, Your comforts delight my soul.

PSALM 94:19 NKJV

"Therefore you now have sorrow; but I will
see you again and your heart will rejoice, and
your joy no one will take from you."

JOHN 16:22 NKJV

"Come to me, all you who are weary and burdened,
and I will give you rest. Take my yoke upon you
and learn from me, for I am gentle and humble in
heart, and you will find rest for your souls."

MATTHEW 11:28–29

*Y*OU ARE READY FOR ANYTHING *and equal to anything* through your living relationship with Me. Rest in My Presence while *I infuse inner strength into you.* Because you are a child of the King of kings, you are capable of so much more than you realize. To benefit fully from your privileged position, however, you need to spend ample time with Me. As you relax in My Presence—delighting in Me and opening your heart to Me—I fill you with inner strength. This time spent together is not only pleasurable, it is empowering.

When there is much to do, it's tempting to rush through your time with Me and dive into the activities of the day. But just as eating a healthy breakfast helps you function at your best, so does feeding your soul a healthy diet of *Me.* Bask in My Word, asking My Spirit to make it come alive to you. Savor these words of Life! Your living relationship with Me helps you approach each new day with confidence—ready for anything that comes your way.

I have strength for all things in Christ Who empowers
me [I am ready for anything and equal to anything
through Him Who infuses inner strength into me;
I am self-sufficient in Christ's sufficiency].

PHILIPPIANS 4:13 AMPC

Delight yourself in the LORD and he will
give you the desires of your heart.

PSALM 37:4

In the morning, O LORD, you hear my voice; in the morning
I lay my requests before you and wait in expectation.

PSALM 5:3

*Y*OU ARE FULLY KNOWN. I know absolutely everything about you, and I love you with perfect, *unfailing Love*. Many people are searching for greater self-understanding and self-acceptance. Underlying their search is a desire to find someone who truly understands them and accepts them as they are. I am the Someone who can fully satisfy this deep-seated longing. It is in your relationship with Me that you discover who you really are.

I encourage you to be real with Me—dropping all pretenses and opening yourself fully to Me. As you draw near, utter these inspired words: *"Search me, O God, and know my heart; test me and know my anxious thoughts."* In the Light of My holy gaze, you will see things you need to change. But don't despair; I will help you. Continue resting in My Presence, receiving My Love that flows freely into you through your openness to Me. Take time to let this powerful Love soak in deeply—filling up your empty spaces and overflowing into joyous worship. Rejoice greatly, for you are fully known and forever loved!

For now we see indistinctly, as in a mirror, but then face to face. Now I know in part, but then I will know fully, as I am fully known.

1 CORINTHIANS 13:12 HCSB

The LORD delights in those who fear him, who put their hope in his unfailing love.

PSALM 147:11

Search me, O God, and know my heart; test me and know my anxious thoughts. See if there is any offensive way in me, and lead me in the way everlasting.

PSALM 139:23–24

I AM PERPETUALLY WITH YOU, taking care of you. That is the most important fact of your existence. I am not limited by time or space; My Presence with you is a forever-promise. You need not fear the future, for I am already there. When you make that quantum leap into eternity, you will find Me awaiting you in heaven. Your future is in My hands; I release it to you day by day, moment by moment. Therefore, *do not worry about tomorrow*.

I want you to live this day abundantly, seeing all there is to see, doing all there is to do. Don't be distracted by future concerns. Leave them to Me! Each day of life is a glorious gift, but so few people know how to live within the confines of today. Much of their energy for abundant living spills over the timeline into tomorrow's worries or past regrets. Their remaining energy is sufficient only for limping through the day, not for living it to the full. I am training you to keep your focus on My Presence in the present. This is how to receive abundant Life, which flows freely from My throne of grace.

"Therefore do not worry about tomorrow,
for tomorrow will worry about itself. Each
day has enough trouble of its own."

MATTHEW 6:34

"The thief comes only to steal and kill
and destroy; I have come that they may
have life, and have it to the full."

JOHN 10:10

Now listen, you who say, "Today or tomorrow we will
go to this or that city, spend a year there, carry on
business and make money." Why, you do not even
know what will happen tomorrow. What is your
life? You are a mist that appears for a little while
and then vanishes. Instead, you ought to say, "If it
is the Lord's will, we will live and do this or that."

JAMES 4:13–15

Trust in Him at all times, you people; pour out your *heart* before Him; God is a *refuge* for us.

<small>PSALM 62:8 NKJV</small>

A Prayer for My Children

_____

_____

_____

_____

_____

_____

_____

_____

_____

_____

_____

_____

*B*EWARE OF OVERTHINKING THINGS—obsessing about unimportant matters. When your mind is idle, you tend to go into planning mode: attempting to figure things out and make various decisions before you really need to do so. This is an unproductive way of trying to grasp control, and it's a waste of your precious time. Often, you end up changing your mind or forgetting what you decided. There is a time for planning, but it's definitely not *all* the time—or even most of it.

Seek to live in the present moment, where My Presence awaits you continually. Refresh yourself in My nearness, letting My Love soak into your innermost being. Relax with Me, putting aside problems so you can be attentive to Me and receive more of My Love. *Your soul thirsts for Me*, but often you don't realize what you're really longing for: awareness of My Presence. Let Me *lead you beside quiet waters* and *restore your soul*. Just as lovers don't need to say much to communicate deeply, so it is in your relationship with Me—the Lover of your soul.

So that Christ may dwell in your hearts through faith.
And I pray that you, being rooted and established in love,
may have power, together with all the saints, to grasp how
wide and long and high and deep is the love of Christ,
and to know this love that surpasses knowledge—that you
may be filled to the measure of all the fullness of God.

EPHESIANS 3:17—19

O God, You are my God; early will I seek You; my
soul thirsts for You; my flesh longs for You in a
dry and thirsty land where there is no water.

PSALM 63:1 NKJV

He makes me lie down in green pastures, he leads me
beside quiet waters, he restores my soul. He guides
me in paths of righteousness for his name's sake.

PSALM 23:2 3

*L*ET ME FILL YOU with My Love, Joy, and Peace. These are Glory-gifts, flowing from My living Presence. Though you are an *earthen vessel*, I designed you to be filled with heavenly contents. Your weakness is not a deterrent to being filled with My Spirit; on the contrary, it provides an opportunity for My Power to shine forth more brightly.

As you go through this day, trust Me to provide the strength you need moment by moment. Don't waste energy wondering whether you are adequate for today's journey. My Spirit within you is more than sufficient to handle whatever this day may bring. That is the basis for your confidence! *In quietness* (spending time alone with Me) *and confident trust* (relying on My sufficiency) *is your strength.*

But we have this treasure in earthen vessels,
so that the surpassing greatness of the power
will be of God and not from ourselves.

2 CORINTHIANS 4:7 NASB

I pray that out of his glorious riches he may strengthen
you with power through his Spirit in your inner being.

EPHESIANS 3:16

This is what the Sovereign LORD, the Holy One of Israel,
says: "In repentance and rest is your salvation, in quietness
and trust is your strength, but you would have none of it."

ISAIAH 30:15

I AM GOOD—*A REFUGE IN TIMES OF TROUBLE. I care for those who trust in Me.* Even though you inhabit a world full of trouble, I assure you that I am completely, 100 percent good! *I am light, and in Me there is no darkness at all.* Seek in Me the perfection you have longed for all your life.

Because of the brokenness of this world, you always need a refuge—but especially *in times of trouble.* When you are hurting, I yearn to shelter you in My powerful, loving Presence. So turn to Me in tough times, and you will find Me faithful.

Many of My children fail to receive My help during difficult times because they don't really trust Me. When adversity strikes, they either lash out angrily at Me or become so focused on their problems that they forget I am with them. An essential element of trusting Me is remembering My promise to *be with you always.* Trust in Me, My child, and I will take care of you.

The Lord is good, a refuge in times of trouble.
He cares for those who trust in him.

NAHUM 1:7

This is the message which we have heard
from Him and declare to you, that God is
light and in Him is no darkness at all.

1 JOHN 1:5 NKJV

"Go and make disciples of all nations, baptizing
them in the name of the Father and of the Son
and of the Holy Spirit, and teaching them to obey
everything I have commanded you. And surely I
am with you always, to the very end of the age."

MATTHEW 28:19–20

When I am *afraid*, I put

my *trust* in you.

PSALM 56:3 ESV

A Prayer for My Children

*T*HOUGH THE MOUNTAINS BE SHAKEN *and the hills be removed, yet My unfailing Love for you will not be shaken nor My covenant of Peace be removed.* Nothing on earth seems as enduring or immovable as soaring, majestic mountains. When you stand on their heights, breathing in that rarified air, you can almost smell eternity. Yet My Love and My Peace are even *more* enduring than the greatest mountain on earth!

Think deeply about *My unfailing Love.* One of the meanings of "unfailing" is *inexhaustible.* No matter how needy you are or how many times you fail Me, My supply of Love for you will never run low. Another meaning of "unfailing" is *constant.* I do not love you more on days when you perform well, nor do I love you less when you fail badly.

I Myself am your Peace. Live close to Me so you can enjoy this supernatural Peace. Come freely into My Presence, beloved, even when you're feeling bad about yourself. Remember who I am: *the Lord who has compassion on you.*

"Though the mountains be shaken and the hills
be removed, yet my unfailing love for you will not
be shaken nor my covenant of peace be removed,"
says the LORD, who has compassion on you.

ISAIAH 54:10

Lift up your eyes to the heavens, look at the earth beneath;
the heavens will vanish like smoke, the earth will wear
out like a garment and its inhabitants die like flies. But my
salvation will last forever, my righteousness will never fail.

ISAIAH 51:6

For He Himself is our peace, who has made both one,
and has broken down the middle wall of separation.

EPHESIANS 2:14 NKJV

I WANT YOU TO EXPERIENCE the riches of your salvation: the Joy of being loved constantly and perfectly. You make a practice of judging yourself based on how you look or behave or feel. If you like what you see in the mirror, you feel a bit more worthy of My Love. When things are going smoothly and your performance seems adequate, you find it easier to believe you are My beloved child. When you feel discouraged, you tend to look inward so you can correct whatever is wrong.

Instead of trying to "fix" yourself, *fix your gaze on Me, the Lover of your soul*. Rather than using your energy to judge yourself, redirect it to praising Me. Remember that I see you clothed in My righteousness, radiant in My perfect Love.

In order that in the coming ages he might show the incomparable riches of his grace, expressed in his kindness to us in Christ Jesus. For it is by grace you have been saved, through faith—and this not from yourselves, it is the gift of God.

EPHESIANS 2:7–8

Therefore, holy brothers, who share in the heavenly calling, fix your thoughts on Jesus, the apostle and high priest whom we confess.

HEBREWS 3:1

Those who look to him are radiant; their faces are never covered with shame.

PSALM 34:5

*T*RUST IN ME FOREVER, FOR I AM THE ROCK ETERNAL. It is easy to trust Me for a while—especially when things are going well in your life. But I am calling you to trust in Me *at all times*, no matter what is happening. I understand what a difficult assignment this is, and I know that you will sometimes fail in this venture. But I continue to love you perfectly even when you don't succeed. Let this assurance of My unfailing Love draw you back to Me—back to trusting Me.

Though your trust is imperfect and unsteady, I am *the Rock eternal*—absolutely steady and unchanging. You can rely on Me! When your walk through this world feels wobbly, remember that I am your Rock. I always provide a stable place for you to stand. I can easily bear all your weight, including the weight of your problems. So come to Me when you are feeling *heavy laden* with worries. I invite you to *lean on Me—trusting Me with all your heart and mind.*

Trust in the Lord forever, for the Lord,
the Lord, is the Rock eternal.

ISAIAH 26:4

"Come to Me, all you who labor and are
heavy laden, and I will give you rest."

MATTHEW 11:28 NKJV

Lean on, trust in, and be confident in the Lord
with all your heart and mind and do not rely
on your own insight or understanding.

PROVERBS 3:5 AMPC

*I*T'S ALL RIGHT TO BE HUMAN. When your mind wanders while you are praying, don't be surprised or upset. Simply return your attention to Me. Share a secret smile with Me, knowing that I understand. Rejoice in My Love for you, which has no limits or conditions. Whisper My Name in loving contentment, assured that *I will never leave you or forsake you.* Intersperse these peaceful interludes abundantly throughout your day. This practice will enable you to attain *a quiet and gentle spirit,* which is pleasing to Me.

As you live in close contact with Me, the Light of My Presence filters through you to bless others. Your weakness and woundedness are the openings through which *the Light of the knowledge of My Glory* shines forth. *My strength and power show themselves most effective in your weakness.*

Be strong and courageous. Do not be afraid or terrified because of them, for the LORD your God goes with you; he will never leave you nor forsake you.

DEUTERONOMY 31:6

For God, who said, "Let light shine out of darkness," made his light shine in our hearts to give us the light of the knowledge of the glory of God in the face of Christ. But we have this treasure in jars of clay to show that this all-surpassing power is from God and not from us.

2 CORINTHIANS 4:6–7

But He said to me . . . My strength and power are made perfect (fulfilled and completed) and show themselves most effective in [your] weakness.

2 CORINTHIANS 12:9 AMPC

Instead, it should be that of your inner self, the unfading *beauty* of a gentle and quiet spirit, which is of great *worth* in God's sight.

1 PETER 3:4

A Prayer for My Children

_____

_____

_____

_____

_____

_____

_____

_____

_____

_____

_____

_____

IVE UP THE ILLUSION of being in control of your life. When things are going smoothly, it's easy to feel as if you're in charge. The more you perceive yourself as your own master, and the more comfortable you become in this role, the harder you will fall.

I want you to enjoy times of smooth sailing and be thankful for them. But don't become addicted to this sense of mastery over your life, and don't consider it the norm. Storms *will* come, and uncertainties will loom on the horizon. If you cling to control and feel entitled to having things go your way, you are likely to sink when difficulties come.

I am training you to *trust in Me at all times—for I am your Refuge.* I use adversity to set you free from the illusion of being in control. When your circumstances and your future are full of uncertainties, look to Me. Find your security in *knowing Me*, the Master who is sovereign over the storms of your life—over everything.

Now listen, you who say, "Today or tomorrow we will go to this or that city, spend a year there, carry on business and make money." Why, you do not even know what will happen tomorrow. What is your life? You are a mist that appears for a little while and then vanishes.

JAMES 4:13—14

Trust in him at all times, O people; pour out your hearts to him, for God is our refuge.

PSALM 62:8

"And this is eternal life, that they may know You, the only true God, and Jesus Christ whom You have sent."

JOHN 17:3 NKJV